T0008104

THE MAGNIFICENT

BOOK OF TREASURES

ANCIENT EGYPT

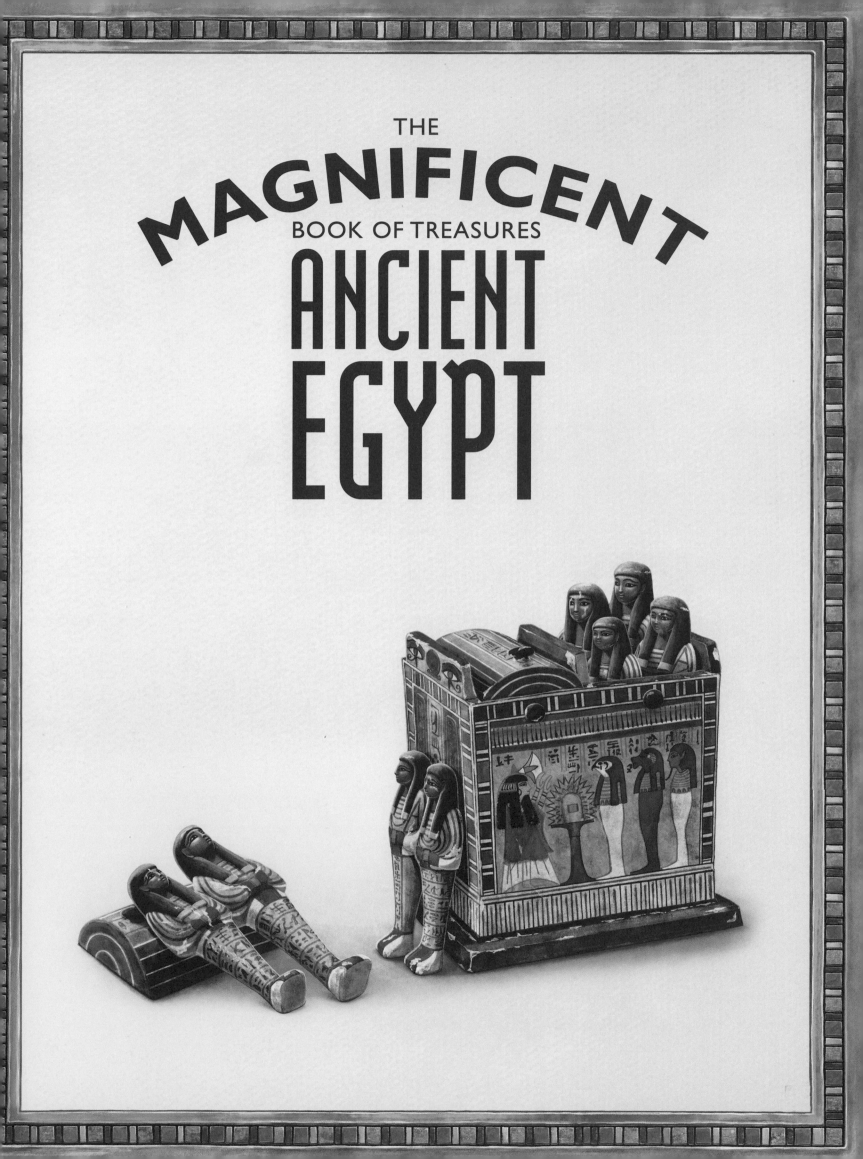

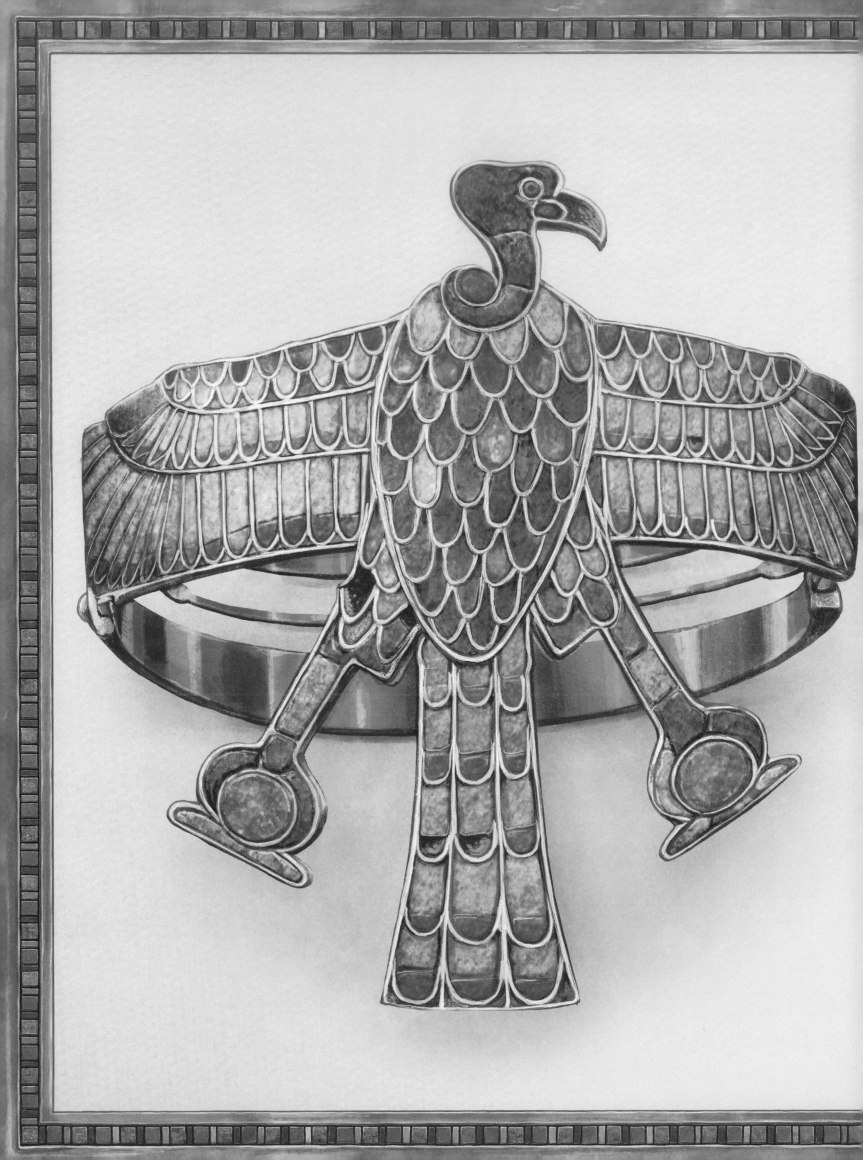

THE MAGNIFICENT

BOOK OF TREASURES

ANCIENT EGYPT

ILLUSTRATED BY **EUGENIA NOBATI**

WRITTEN BY **PHILIP STEELE**

Written by Philip Steele
Illustrated by Eugenia Nobati
Consultant: Dr. Loretta Kilroe

Copyright © Weldon Owen International, L.P. 2021

All rights reserved. No part of this publication may be
reproduced, distributed, or transmitted in any form or by
any means, including photocopying, recording, or other
electronic or mechanical methods, without the prior
written permission of the publisher, except in the case of
brief quotations embodied in critical reviews and certain
other noncommercial uses permitted by copyright law.

Published by Weldon Owen Children's Books
An imprint of Weldon Owen International, L.P.
A subsidiary of Insight International, L.P.
PO Box 3088
San Rafael, CA 94912
www.insighteditions.com

Weldon Owen Children's Books:
Designed by Bryn Walls
Edited by Diana Craig
Assistant Editor: Pandita Geary
Senior Production Manager: Greg Steffen
Art Director: Stuart Smith
Publisher: Sue Grabham

Insight Editions:
Publisher: Raoul Goff

ISBN: 978-1-68188-558-2
Manufactured, printed, and assembled in China
First printing, September 2021. STR/09/21
25 24 23 22 2 3 4 5

INTRODUCTION

Egypt is a land of sandy deserts, which bake and shimmer in the blistering heat. Few people would have settled here if it hadn't been for the river Nile. This great waterway gave the ancient Egyptians water for drinking and a route for boats. When it flooded, it provided rich, fertile soil for farming. The civilization that grew up around the Nile began in about 5500 BCE and lasted for thousands of years. During that time, the Egyptians created some of the most beautiful objects and art in the world.

The Magnificent Book of Treasures Ancient Egypt takes you into this long-forgotten world and shines a light on its mysteries. Marvel at the golden mask of the boy-king Tutankhamun and the gold sandals placed on his mummified feet. Meet some of the most powerful Egyptian queens, such as Tiye and Nefertiti. Learn about the sun god Ra, the cat goddess Bastet, and the mother goddess Hathor.

Find out what the ancient Egyptians believed happened to people after they died. Learn why they placed little models of boatmen, bakers, and farmers in their tombs, and why they buried their dead with books of spells. See a table laid out for a princess, a royal lucky charm, and the mummy of a cat.

Embark on a journey into the past to discover some of the most magnificent ancient Egyptian treasures ever found.

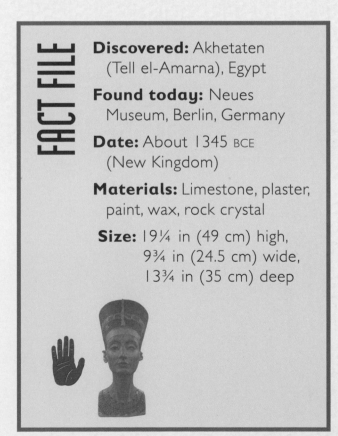

FACT FILE

Discovered: Akhetaten (Tell el-Amarna), Egypt

Found today: Neues Museum, Berlin, Germany

Date: About 1345 BCE (New Kingdom)

Materials: Limestone, plaster, paint, wax, rock crystal

Size: 19¼ in (49 cm) high, 9¾ in (24.5 cm) wide, 13¾ in (35 cm) deep

CONTENTS

A PRINCESS'S COFFINS

- The ancient Egyptians often made coffins that fit inside each other, like Russian dolls. The coffins protected the dead person during their journey to the next world. This set belonged to Princess Henettawy (*Henna-tah-we*).

- Henettawy was known as the Singer of Amun-R. She served as an important priestess in Amun-Ra's temple. This god was the greatest of them all. He was said to sail across the sky every day in a boat, wearing the sun disk on his head.

- Two coffins and a flat "mummy board" make up Henettawy's coffin set. They are all shaped like mummies. The princess's body was wrapped in linen bandages, placed inside the inner coffin, and covered with the board.

- Henettawy's face is painted on the front of both coffins and the board. This was to help guide her spirit back if she wanted to rejoin the world of the living.

- The inner coffin is painted to look like gold. It shows Osiris (*Oh-sy-ris*), the god of death and rebirth. His green skin represents the plants that die and grow again. His wife Isis (*Eye-sis*) spreads her wings across both coffins and the board.

- The outer coffin is painted white like the wrappings of a mummy. Prayers, good luck charms, and pictures of gods and goddesses cover the surface. These are all there to help the princess reach the next world.

FACT FILE

Discovered: Near Thebes (Luxor), Egypt

Found today: Metropolitan Museum of Art, New York City, USA

Date: 1000–945 BCE (Third Intermediate Period)

Materials: Wood, paint

Size: Outer coffin 80 in (203 cm) long, inner coffin 75 in (191 cm) long, mummy board 67½ in (171.3 cm) long

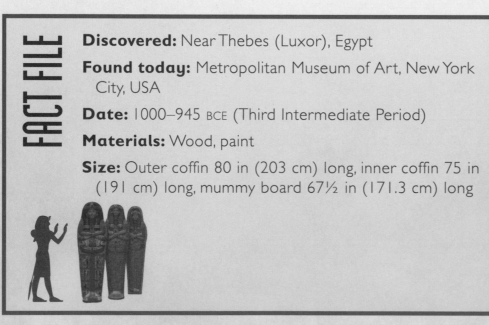

BOAT OF THE DEAD

➤ This model boat is carrying an important passenger. His name is Meketre (*Me-ket-ra*), and he is sitting under the canopy in the middle. Meketre is on his final journey to the Underworld, where his spirit will live on after he dies.

- The ancient Egyptians placed model boats like this in people's tombs. They believed that this would help the spirits of the dead to travel to the Underworld to meet Osiris (*Oh-sy-ris*), the god of death.

- This model is made of painted wood. Sixteen little wooden oarsmen with paddles are rowing it, and two figures at the back are steering with two long rudders.

- The real Meketre lived about 4,000 years ago. He was an important official who worked for the pharaohs who ruled Egypt. The model boat was found in a secret chamber of his tomb.

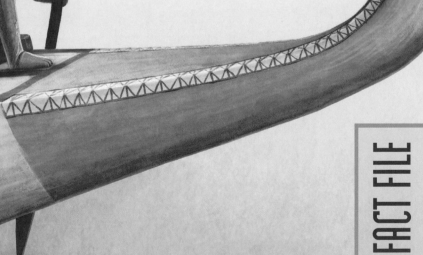

FACT FILE

Discovered: Near Thebes (Luxor), Egypt

Found today: Metropolitan Museum of Art, New York, USA

Date: 1981–1975 BCE (Middle Kingdom)

Materials: Wood, paint, plaster, linen

Size: 54 in (138 cm) long, 21 in (53 cm) high, 15 in (38 cm) wide

HUNTING IN THE MARSHES

- In this painting, a man called Nebamun (*Nebba-mun*) is shown enjoying himself out hunting in the marshes around the Nile.

- Nebamun is holding a throwing stick, which was a kind of boomerang. It was used to bring down large water birds, such as wild ducks and geese.

- By his side in the boat, Nebamun's wife and daughter look on. Even his cat is there, hunting birds. The cat's eye is painted in gold, so it may represent the sun god.

- Nebamun's little boat is made from bundles of reeds tied together. They come from a plant called papyrus, which grows beside the River Nile.

- This scene does not show Nebamun when he was alive, but in his next life, after death. It was painted on the wall of his tomb.

- When he was alive, Nebamun was an important official at the temple of Amun, the greatest of all the Egyptian gods.

FACT FILE

Discovered: Near Thebes (Luxor), Egypt

Found today: British Museum, London, England

Date: About 1350 BCE (New Kingdom)

Materials: Plaster, paint

Size: 32¾ in (83 cm) high, 38½ in (98 cm) wide

A LIVING GODDESS

- Nefertiti (*Neffer-tee-tee*) was one of the most powerful queens in the history of Egypt. Her name means "the beautiful one has arrived."

- The royal sculptor Thutmose (*Toot-moh-suh*) made this model of the queen's head in his workshop.

- The model was made by carefully smoothing plaster over a limestone base. The eyes are made from wax and rock crystal.

- Thutmose added a collar of many colors and a crown of blue and gold to his statue of the queen.

- The queen's fine features are painted in delicate colors. Thutmose may have used this very realistic head as a model for students of painting.

- Queen Nefertiti was the chief wife of a pharaoh called Akhenaten (*Ah-ken-ah-ten*). She had six daughters.

Nefertiti was a living goddess. She and her husband worshipped Aten instead of all the other Egyptian gods and goddesses. Aten's symbol was a sun disk.

This statue made Nefertiti famous. She is as well-known as her stepson, the pharaoh Tutankhamun (*Tut-ank-amun*).

FACT FILE

Discovered: Akhetaten (Tell el-Amarna), Egypt

Found today: Neues Museum, Berlin, Germany

Date: About 1345 BCE (New Kingdom)

Materials: Limestone, plaster, paint, wax, rock crystal

Size: 19¼ in (49 cm) high, 9¾ in (24.5 cm) wide, 13¾ in (35 cm) deep

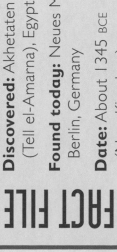

THE BLUE HIPPO

➤ This little hippopotamus was placed in a tomb in southern Egypt about 4,000 years ago. A royal official called Senbi was buried there.

➤ The hippo is one of two that were found in the tomb. Both hippos were modeled from a type of pottery called faience, with a shiny blue glaze.

- Lotus flowers are painted on the hippo's body. These flowers are also known as water lilies. They grow in the mud of the river Nile.

- The Egyptians believed that lotus flowers were magical symbols of rebirth because they close at night and reopen in the day. The flowers on Senbi's hippos were meant to help him enter the next world after his death.

- Hippos were a common sight in ancient Egypt. They could be dangerous neighbors. They often overturned small boats on the river. By night they rampaged through the fields, uprooting the crops.

- Ancient Egyptians hunted hippos using harpoons and ropes.

- Egyptians admired the way that hippos protected their young. Statues of Taweret (*Ta-wer-et*), the goddess of childbirth, are shaped like hippos.

- This little hippo now lives in a museum in New York City. He is nicknamed William and is a favorite with many visitors.

FACT FILE

Discovered: Meir, near Asyut, Egypt

Found today: Metropolitan Museum of Art, New York City, USA

Date: 1968–1878 BCE (Middle Kingdom)

Materials: Glazed pottery (faience), paint

Size: 7¾ in (20 cm) long, 3 in (7.5 cm) wide, 4½ in (11.2 cm) high

THE MAGIC SONS OF HORUS

- The ancient Egyptians believed that people still needed certain body organs in the afterlife. Before they mummified a body, they removed the lungs, liver, stomach, and bowels and preserved them in jars that looked like these.

- The jars are known as canopic jars. They were buried with the dead person whose organs they contained. The little figures here are wooden copies of those jars.

- Each figure looks like one of the four sons of the god Horus (*Haw-rus*). These gods protected the four different parts of the body that were once buried inside the jars.

- Qebehsenuef (*Ke-beh-sen-oo-ef*) had the head of a falcon and was the god of the west. He was the guardian of the bowels.

- With his baboon head, Hapy (*Hay-pee*) was the god of the north. He kept watch over the lungs.

FACT FILE

Discovered: Near Thebes (Luxor), Egypt

Found today: The Louvre Museum, Paris, France

Date: 1069–747 BCE

Materials: Wood, paint

Size: 12¾ in (32.5 cm) high, 5½ in (13.6 cm) wide

- Jackal-headed Duamutef (*Doo-amoo-tef*) was the god of the east. He was the guardian of the stomach.

- Imsety (*Im-setee*) had a human head and was the god of the south. He was the protector of the liver.

THE PHARAOH'S GOLDEN MASK

- This precious mask is made of gleaming gold and decorated with beautiful stones and colored glass. It was placed over the face of the mummy of a pharaoh called Tutankhamun (*Tut-ank-amun*).

- Tutankhamun became pharaoh, or king of Egypt, when he was only about nine years old. When he died eleven years later, his body was preserved as a mummy.

- The striped headcloth is topped by a cobra and a vulture. These animals represented Upper (southern) and Lower (northern) Egypt. They show that Tutankhamun ruled the whole country, all the way from the north to the south.

- The Egyptians believed that the pharaohs were living gods, so the mask has been made to look godlike. It has the face of the god Osiris (*Oh-sy-ris*). The gold shines like the sun god, Ra. It has a false beard, which was sacred to the gods.

- A magic spell was written on the back of the mask to protect the pharaoh from evil spirits.

- Tutankhamun was buried in a secret underground tomb. The tomb was packed with 5,398 treasures and supplies, which the king could use when he traveled to the next world, or the afterlife.

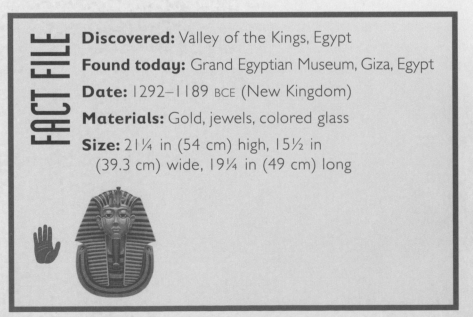

FACT FILE

Discovered: Valley of the Kings, Egypt

Found today: Grand Egyptian Museum, Giza, Egypt

Date: 1292–1189 BCE (New Kingdom)

Materials: Gold, jewels, colored glass

Size: 21¼ in (54 cm) high, 15½ in (39.3 cm) wide, 19¼ in (49 cm) long

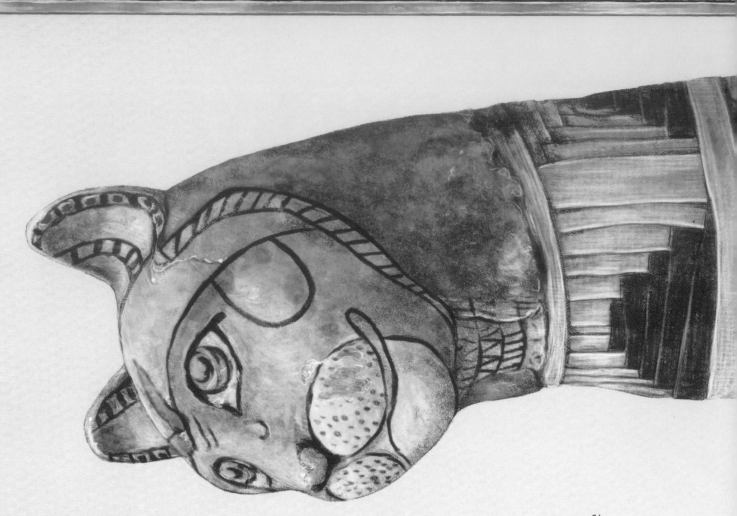

MUMMY OF A CAT

◆ The ancient Egyptians made mummies of animals as well as humans. They mummified baboons, crocodiles, birds, fish, and pet cats like the one shown here.

◆ Favorite pets were sometimes mummified after death so that they could travel to the next world. It was believed that they would meet the spirits of their owners there.

◆ Some animals could be helpful to their owners in the afterlife, just as they were in the world of the living. A pet cat could make itself useful by catching mice.

◆ Most animal mummies were not prepared as carefully as humans were. They were just preserved in sticky resin and bandaged up in coarse linen.

◆ The remains of this cat have been neatly wrapped in strips of cloth. Its face has been painted on, rather like the face on a stuffed toy.

◆ Huge numbers of cat mummies have been discovered at Bubastis in northern Egypt. People went to Bubastis to make offerings to Bastet, the cat goddess.

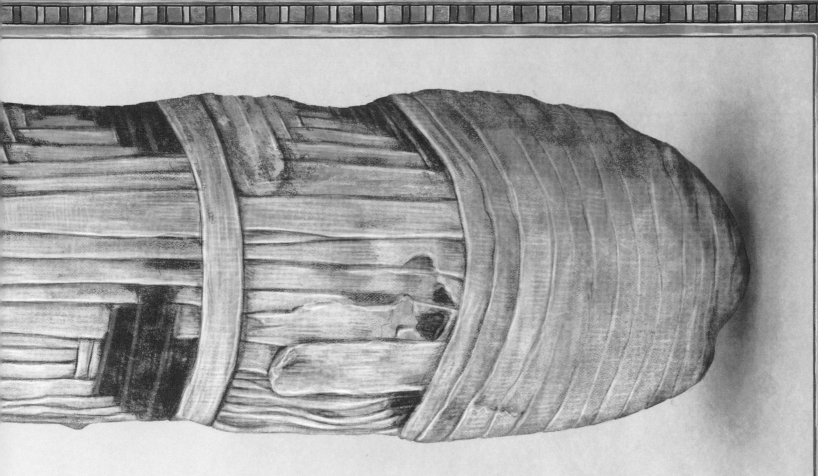

- Many Egyptian gods were closely linked to animals and are often shown with animal heads. People believed that these creatures were very holy, or sacred.

- Sacred animals were often mummified at temples and offered as gifts to the gods. Sometimes these mummies were just bundles of bones and rubbish made into animal shapes.

FACT FILE

Discovered: Possibly Bubastis, Egypt

Found today: The Louvre Museum, Paris, France

Date: 664–332 BCE

Materials: Mummified cat, linseed oil, cloth, paint

Size: 15¼ in (39 cm) high, 3¾ in (9.7 cm) wide, head depth 4 in (10.4 cm)

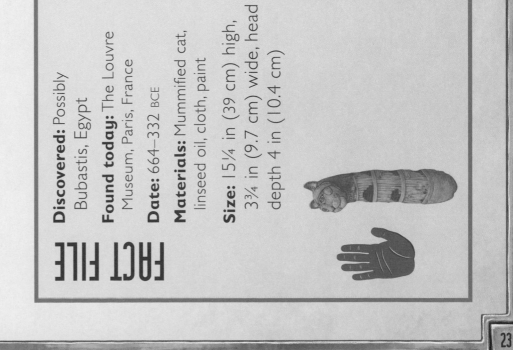

EGYPTIAN BAKERY

◆ The Egyptians grew barley and a type of wheat called emmer. These grains were used to bake bread and to brew beer. The model shows people at work in a bakery, crushing and grinding grain, kneading dough, and tending the oven.

◆ This model was placed in the tomb of Meketre (*Me-ket-ra*), an important official from Thebes, about 4,000 years ago. With bakers like these at hand, he would never need to go hungry in the next world.

- The ancient Egyptians knew how to use yeast to make bread dough rise. Loaves were often baked in molds. They came in all shapes and sizes, from cones to domes.

- Egyptian bakers sweetened bread with honey, figs, or dates or flavored it with nuts and spices. They baked cakes and pastries that were shaped like people or crocodiles.

- In ancient Egypt, the flour that bakers used was often gritty. This explains why many ancient Egyptians had worn-down teeth.

FACT FILE

Discovered: Near Thebes (Luxor), Egypt

Found today: Metropolitan Museum of Art, New York City, USA

Date: 1981–1975 BCE (Middle Kingdom)

Materials: Wood, paint

Size: Tallest baker 7 in (18 cm) high

THRONE OF GOLD

- This royal throne is covered in gold. It glitters with silver, bronze, gems, and colored glass. The pharaoh Tutankhamun (*Tut-ank-amun*) sat here to give out orders and to meet important people and visitors from distant lands.

- Tutankhamun was the son of Akhenaten (*Ah-ken-ah-ten*), a pharaoh who brought in a new religion. He worshipped only one god called Aten, whose symbol was a sun disk. Aten's disk shines on the back of the throne.

- The backrest shows Tutankhamun with his wife, Ankhesenamun (*Ank-es-en-amun*). They wear crowns, wigs, fine linen, and jeweled collars. The queen is rubbing the king's shoulder with perfumed oil from a dish in her hand.

- The lotus flowers and papyrus reeds on the backrest symbolize southern and northern Egypt. They show that Tutankhamun ruled the whole country.

- Winged cobras decorate the armrests. The cobra was a symbol of royal power. The legs of the throne represent the eastern and western borders of Egypt. They are guarded by fierce lions.

FACT FILE

Discovered: Near Thebes (Luxor), Egypt

Found today: Grand Egyptian Museum, Giza, Egypt

Date: About 1336 BCE (New Kingdom)

Materials: Wood, gold, silver, semi-precious stones, colored glass, glazed pottery (faience)

Size: 40 in (102 cm) high, 21¼ in (54 cm) wide, 23½ in (60 cm) deep

THE BRINGER OF FOOD

- As she strides along, this little statue balances a basket on her head. Inside the basket are supplies of meat and loaves of bread. She holds a duck in her right hand.

- This statue is beautifully carved and painted in rich colors. The woman is clearly not a poor servant or farm girl. She wears jewelery and a fine dress with a beaded pattern.

- The ancient Egyptians believed that the spirits of the dead lived on in the next world, so they needed to eat and drink. This woman is bringing food to a tomb to give to the spirit of the dead person.

- This was one of two statues placed in a tomb nearly 4,000 years ago. They may have represented the goddesses Nepthys (Neff-thiss) and Isis (Eye-sis), who were believed to protect the dead.

- The tomb where this statue was found belonged to a very important man called Meketre (Me-ket-ra). He was an official at the royal court for many years.

- Inside Meketre's tomb was a hidden chamber that was full of little statues. As well as this statue, there were models of workshops, gardens, and boats.

- Tomb models like this one were meant to help the dead person live a good life in the next world. Today, they can tell us how people lived from day to day in ancient Egypt.

FACT FILE

Discovered: Thebes (Luxor), Egypt

Found today: Metropolitan Museum of Art, New York City, USA

Date: 1981–1975 BCE

Materials: Wood, paint

Size: 44 in (112 cm) high, 6¾ in (17 cm) wide, 18½ in (46.7 cm) deep

MUSIC FOR A GOD

- In this painting, a musician runs his fingers over the strings of his harp. The sweet notes he plays ring out through the temple. The hieroglyphs, or writing, tell us that he is singing a hymn called "Adore Ra When He Rises."

- This scene was painted on a wooden stele, or slab. The harpist kneels before the falcon-headed god Ra-Horakhty (*Ra-haw-rak-ty*), who sits on a throne in all his glory. Ra-Horakhty was lord of the sky and the rising sun.

- This harpist served as a powerful high priest at the temple of Amun in Thebes. The artist wanted to paint him praising the gods to show people that the harpist was a good and religious person.

- Ordinary people were not allowed to join in the worship inside Egyptian temples. That was left to priests, priestesses, and musicians. They offered food to the gods, burned incense, and filled the air with music and singing.

- The Egyptians loved to make all sorts of music with bells, rattles, and cymbals. They played flutes and oboes too, as well as harps and lyres.

- Music was popular at royal feasts. Dancers and acrobats would clap, shake tambourines, and tap out rhythms as they performed.

- Trumpets and drums were often played by Egyptian soldiers as they marched to war.

FACT FILE

Discovered: Thebes (Luxor), Egypt

Found today: The Louvre Museum, Paris, France

Date: About 1045 BCE (Third Intermediate Period)

Materials: Wood, limestone, paint

Size: 11½ in (29.5 cm) high, 8¾ in (22.4 cm) wide

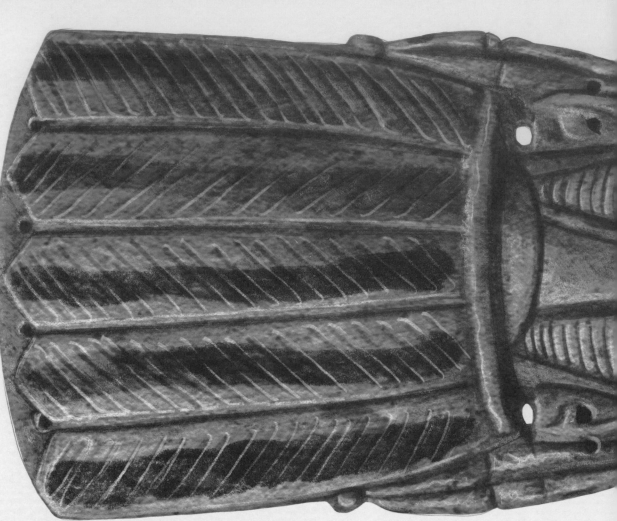

THE LITTLE GREEN GOD

◆ This little green man is a statue of the god Bes. He looks more like a fierce demon than a god. Sometimes Bes is shown with a big, fat belly and a stuck-out tongue.

◆ In ancient Egypt, Bes appeared on jewelery, spoons, mirrors, and lucky charms and in wall paintings. Jars were made in the shape of his head.

◆ This figure is made of glassy green faience, a special type of glazed pottery. Details have been added in black paint.

◆ The god is sitting on a lotus, or water lily, with a monkey between his feet. He wears a feather headdress. In his arms, he cradles a baby version of himself.

◆ Bes was believed to protect women when they gave birth. He looked after families, guarded the home, and kept away dangers such as snakes.

- This little green god is often shown playing a musical instrument or dancing. He was once seen as a god of war and was sometimes shown holding knives.

- Bes may have started out as an African god in the lands south of Egypt. His popularity spread, and he was worshipped as far away as Persia (modern Iran).

- The god Bes did not always appear as a little green man. Sometimes he was shown as a lion or a dwarf.

FACT FILE

Discovered: Tuna el-Gebel, near Mallawi, Egypt

Found today: British Museum, London, UK

Date: 664–332 BCE (Late Period)

Materials: Glazed pottery (faience), paint

Size: 8 in (20.2 cm) high, 3 in (7.5 cm) wide

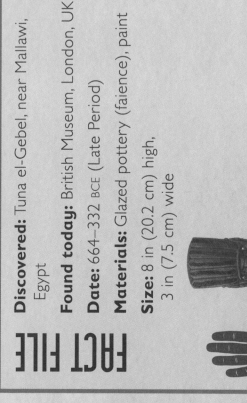

ANIMAL BOARD GAME

- Board games were as popular in ancient Egypt as they are today. This model gaming table was found at Thebes in the tomb of a pharaoh called Amenemhat (*Ah-mennim-hat*).

- This tiny table is made of ivory, or animal tusks, and a wood called ebony. The top is painted with a palm tree design. The carved legs end in hooves, like a bull's.

- The animal-headed pins were used to play this game. Five have dogs' heads and five have jackals' heads. The pins slot into the holes on the board and can be stored in the drawer.

- The rules of this game are not known, but the two players probably raced their pieces to the finishing point. They may have decided the moves by throwing dice, bones, or sticks.

- A *shen* sign marks the finishing point on top of this board. A shen is an unbroken circle of rope, and it shows that a task has been completed safely.

- The Egyptians may have placed board games in tombs to symbolize the spirit's journey. Traveling to the afterlife was a bit like a board game, with many challenges along the way.

FACT FILE

Discovered: Thebes (Luxor), Egypt

Found today: Metropolitan Museum of Art, New York City, USA

Date: 1814–1805 BCE (Middle Kingdom)

Materials: Wood, paint

Size: Table 2¾ in (6.8 cm) high, 6 in (15.6 cm) long, 4 in (10.1cm) wide; Jackal pins 2¾–3½ in (7–8.5 cm) high; Hound pins 2¼–2¾ in (6–6.8 cm) high.

THE GOLDEN BUCKLE

- A chariot returns from the battlefield. It is pulled by two galloping horses and is driven by the pharaoh Tutankhamun (*Tut-ank-amun*). His hound races alongside. They all appear on a buckle belonging to Tutankhamun.

- This scene was worked in fine gold by a master craftsman more than 3,000 years ago. The buckle was found in Tutankhamun's tomb.

The buckle shows Tutankahmun standing alone in an open-backed chariot with two wooden wheels. His bow is inside a case, full of arrows. His horses are fitted out with fancy coats, harnesses, and ostrich plumes.

Egyptian artists liked to show pharaohs riding chariots alongside the enemies they had defeated and the prisoners they had captured. That is how Tutankhamun appears here.

Tutankhamun did not fight any battles in real life. The scene on this buckle was just meant to show him as a powerful ruler.

There were four real chariots in Tutankhmun's tomb.

FACT FILE

Discovered: Near Thebes (Luxor)

Found today: Grand Egyptian Museum, Giza, Egypt

Date: 1327 BCE (New Kingdom)

Material: Gold

Size: 3¾ in (9.7 cm) wide

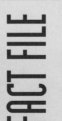

THE PALACE GARDEN

- The ancient Egyptians often carved and painted beautiful pictures on slabs of limestone like this one. The painting shows a man and a woman dressed in fine pleated linen and wearing splendid collars.

- Both figures wear a model cobra above their foreheads. The cobra was a symbol of royalty, so we know that the man and woman are a pharaoh and a queen.

- The royal couple were busy and important people, but here they look very relaxed. They could be out walking in the palace gardens. The queen is holding out a bunch of lotus flowers for the king to smell.

- This realistic style of art was popular around the reign of the pharaoh Akhenaten (*Ah-ken-ah-ten*).

- It is thought that this royal couple are the pharaoh Tutankamun (*Tut-ank-amun*) and his wife Ankhesenamun (*Ank-ess-en-amun*). Before she became queen, Ankhesenamun was a royal princess.

- Akhenaten brought in a new religion that worshipped only one god called Aten instead of all the old gods. He also built a new capital city at Tell el-Amarna. That is where this painting was found.

FACT FILE

Discovered: Tell el-Amarna, Egypt

Found today: Neues Museum, Berlin, Germany

Date: About 1335 BCE (New Kingdom)

Materials: Limestone, paint

Size: 9¾ in (24.8 cm) high, 8 in (20 cm) wide, 2½ in (6.5 cm) deep

SERVANTS OF THE DEAD

- This box of eight *shabti* figures was buried with a priestess called Henutmehyt (*Hen-ut-mehite*). She worshipped in the temple of Amun-Ra, who was god of the universe, the sun, and the air.

- Shabtis were the servants of the dead. They were buried in tombs so that they could work for the dead forever in the afterlife.

- Egyptians believed that shabtis would be magically brought to life in the next world by a spell from the Book of the Dead.

- The job of a shabti was written on its front in ancient Egyptian writing called hieroglyphics.

FACT FILE

Discovered: Thebes (Luxor), Egypt

Found today: British Museum, London, UK

Date: 1292–1189 BCE (New Kingdom)

Materials: Wood, paint

Size: 13¾ in (35 cm) high, 7½ in (19.2 cm) wide, 13½ in (34 cm) long

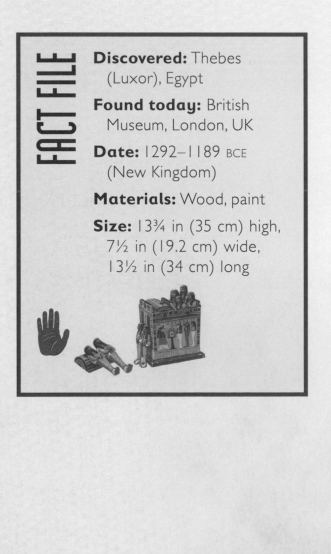

The painting of Henutmehyt on the side of the box shows her with a lotus flower in her hair. This is a sign that she will come back to life in the next world, just like the lotus that closes at night but opens at dawn.

Henutmehyt is shown worshipping three gods, praying to them to protect her soul on its journey to the Underworld.

QUEEN WITH A CROWN OF FEATHERS

◆ Tiye (Tee-yay) was a great queen who lived more than 3,000 years ago. This small model of her head is made of yew wood, with eyes of ebony wood and a white stone called alabaster.

◆ This strong, intelligent woman was the daughter of a priestess and an important official. Her parents' families may have come from a region called Nubia, to the south of Egypt.

◆ The pharaoh Amenhotep III (Ah-men-ho-tep) married Tiye and she became queen of Egypt. She was called the Great Royal Wife, and she and her husband ruled Egypt together.

◆ The queen had several official names. They included Mistress of the Two Lands because she ruled Upper and Lower Egypt. Tiye wielded enormous power.

◆ Tiye's son Akhenaten (Ah-ken-ah-ten) became king after his father, Amenhotep, died. Tiye still held an important place in the royal court after her son took the throne.

◆ This model head once had a gold headdress. There was a golden cobra in front, where the two gold clips are. The cobra was a symbol of important royalty.

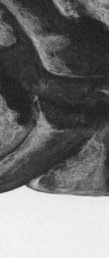

- The sun disk and cow's horns on the headdress are symbols of Hathor, goddess of the sky, women, fertility, and love. Some people believed that Tiye represented Hathor.

- The two tall feathers of Tiye's crown show that she is to be honored as a goddess.

- Queen Tiye was the grandmother of the famous pharaoh Tutankamun (*Tut-ank-amun*).

FACT FILE

Discovered: Medinet Ghurab, Egypt

Found today: Neues Museum, Berlin, Germany

Date: About 1350 BCE (New Kingdom)

Materials: Yew wood, silver, gold, glazed pottery (faience)

Size: 8¾ in (22.5 cm) high

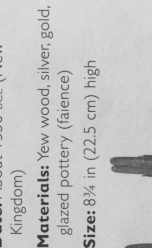

GARDEN OF DELIGHTS

- Egypt is a land of deserts and burning sun. ancient Egyptians built walled gardens like this one, where they could relax away from the heat. The gardens were cool and shady, with rippling pools of water.

- This wall painting is more than 3,000 years old. It shows what the beautiful gardens of rich Egyptians looked like.

- The garden in this picture was painted on the wall of a tomb belonging to a man called Nebamun (*Nebba-mun*). The garden was meant to be ready for him in the next world, after he died.

- The pool in the center of the garden is filled with fish, ducks, and water lilies. Around it grow sweet-scented flowers and herbs. The trees are shady, and their leaves rustle in the breeze.

- A feast of fruits fills the garden, waiting for Nebamun to pick them. Juicy figs hang from the fig trees, the palm trees are laden with dates, and the doum palms are heavy with nuts.

FACT FILE

Discovered: Near Thebes (Luxor), Egypt

Found today: British Museum, London, UK

Date: About 1350 BCE (New Kingdom)

Materials: Plaster, paint

Size: 25 in (64 cm) high, 28¾ in (73 cm) wide

- To the right of the pool, Nebamun's wife waits to welcome him to the delights of the next world with offerings of fruit and drink.

- This picture was painted on plaster. The colors were originally brighter, but the blues and greens have faded over time.

SOUL HOUSE

- This little clay model may look like a dolls' house, but it is really part of a tray to be placed on a dead person's tomb. Relatives or priests would leave offerings on the tray to help the person on their journey to the next world.

- A soul house reminded people that the tomb was a home for the soul, or spirit, of the dead person. Clay models of foods such as bread, fish, and vegetables lie in front of the house to give the soul something to eat.

- This soul house is only a rough model, but it can tell us about real Egyptian homes. They were built from brick and had a large main room that opened out onto a yard or the street.

- Like a real Egyptian home, this soul house has stairs leading up to a flat roof. This was where people might sit and talk in the evening, or sleep at night.

- The soul house has a window, an arched porch, and an air vent on the flat roof. In real Egyptian homes, these would allow cooling breezes to blow through.

FACT FILE

Discovered: Possibly near Thebes (Luxor), Egypt

Found today: British Museum, London, UK

Date: 1985–1795 BCE (Middle Kingdom)

Material: Clay

Size: 7 in (17.5 cm) high, 16 in (41 cm) wide, 15 in (38 cm) deep

SEATED SCRIBE

- A scribe is somebody who writes things down. Few people in ancient Egypt could read or write, so the job was very important. This model of a scribe is about 4,400 years old.

- Scribes wrote with brushes or pens made of reeds. They used blocks of dried red or black ink, a palette, and a water pot. This figure may have held a brush or pen in his right hand.

- The ancient Egyptians did not have paper. Scribes wrote on papyrus instead. This was like a thick paper made from the stems of the papyrus plant. A length of papyrus rests on this figure's lap.

- Scribes like this one wrote in a flowing script called hieratic. It is different from the hieroglyphic picture symbols we see in tombs and temples.

- In ancient Egypt, this scribe would been known as a *sesh*. This name meant much more than just "writer." The word also described clerks, accountants, and high officials from estates, palaces, or temples.

FACT FILE

Discovered: Saqqara, west of modern Cairo, Egypt

Found today: Grand Egyptian Museum, Giza, Egypt

Date: 2494–2345 BCE (Old Kingdom)

Materials: Limestone, paint

Size: 20 in (50.8 cm) high

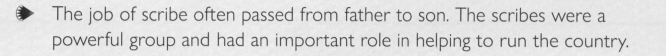

The job of scribe often passed from father to son. The scribes were a powerful group and had an important role in helping to run the country.

THE EYE OF HORUS

- The pharaoh Tutankhamun (*Tut-ank-amun*) may have worn this pendant when he was alive as an amulet or lucky charm. It was found with his mummy.

- The eye on this pendant was known as a *wedjat* eye. It represented the magic eye of the god Horus (*Haw-rus*). Egyptian amulets were full of secret meanings.

- The Eye of Horus had the power to heal and protect It gained this power after Horus lost it in a fight with the god Seth. It was later repaired by the god Thoth.

- This *wedjat* eye is made of blue and red glass paste edged with gold. It hangs from strings of beads made from gold, blue faience, a blue stone called lapis lazuli, and a red stone called carnelian.

- Two small figures are holding the eye. They are known as the Nebty, or the Two Ladies of Egypt.

- The vulture on the left of the eye represents the goddess Nekhbet (*Neck-bet*). She wears a tall, feathered crown and was the guardian of Upper Egypt.

FACT FILE

Discovered: Near Thebes (Luxor), Egypt

Found today: Grand Egyptian Museum, Giza, Egypt

Date: 1370–1352 BCE (New Kingdom)

Materials: Gold, glass paste, glazed pottery (faience), lapis lazuli, carnelian

Size: 2¼ in (5.7 cm) wide

The cobra with a tall crown on the right of the eye represents a goddess called Wedjat. She protected Lower Egypt. The cobra was also a symbol of royal power.

The Egyptians believed that this magic eye and the two goddesses would protect Tutankhamun and guide him safely to his new life in the next world.

THE LITTLE PLOWMAN

◗ This model figure is plowing the soil and preparing it for sowing. He is standing ankle-deep in mud left by the river Nile. The great river flooded once a year.

◗ Most of the year, Egypt was too hot and dry for growing crops. But when the Nile flooded, the rich soil it left behind was perfect for farming. Then laborers like this went to work the land.

◗ The plowman is dressed only in a simple linen kilt. Pushing a plow under the Egyptian sun was hot work.

◗ The plow is a simple one, made of wood but with a metal blade to turn the soil. It is hauled by two black-and-white oxen.

FACT FILE

Discovered: Possibly Memphis (Cairo) area, Egypt

Found today: British Museum, London, UK

Date: 1985–1795 BCE (Middle Kingdom)

Materials: Wood, paint

Size: 8 in (20.3 cm) high, 7 in (17.7 cm) wide, 17 in (43.2 cm) long

The Nile floods were so important to the Egyptians that they told a story about them. They said that the floodwaters were really the tears of the great goddess Isis (*Eye-sis*), weeping for her dead husband, the god Osiris (*Oh-sy-ris*).

Models like this one were placed in the tombs of rich landowners and officials. This was meant to give the dead a way of producing all the food they needed in the next world.

IN MEMORY OF A QUEEN

- This wall painting shows Queen Ahmose-Nefertari (*Ah-moss-neffer-tar-ree*). She was a priestess of the god Amun.

- Ahmose-Nefertari's painting was found in the tomb of a man called Kynebu (*Kin-eh-boo*), who was a priest of Amun.

- Ahmose-Nefertari lived 400 years before Kynebu. But her portrait appears in his tomb as a way of honoring her.

- The headdress the figure wears is made up of a sun disk with ostrich feathers. This is a royal headdress, worn by queens.

- The cobra symbol on the queen's head and the flail, or whip, in her right hand are both signs of royalty.

- In her left hand, Ahmose-Nefertari holds a lotus flower. This flower closes at night but opens again the next morning, so it symbolizes rebirth.

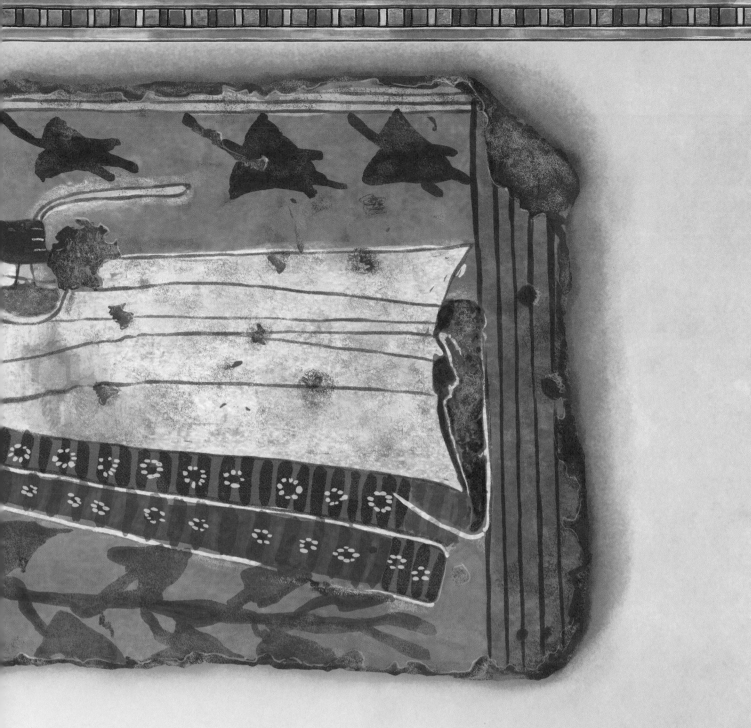

Ahmose-Nefertari held great power. She was one of the most important women in Egyptian history. After she died, she was worshipped as a goddess.

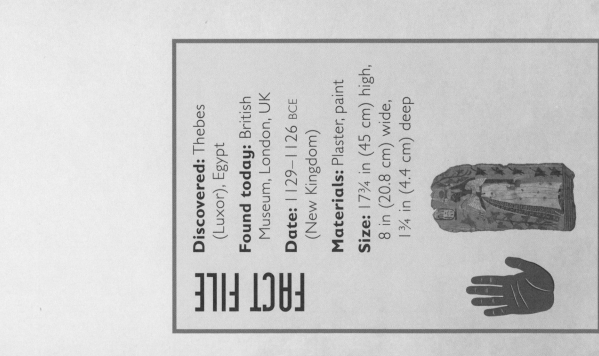

FACT FILE

Discovered: Thebes (Luxor), Egypt

Found today: British Museum, London, UK

Date: 1129–1126 BCE (New Kingdom)

Materials: Plaster, paint

Size: 17¾ in (45 cm) high, 8 in (20.8 cm) wide, 1¾ in (4.4 cm) deep

A GAME OF CHANCE

- The Egyptians loved to play board games, and their favorite was called *senet*. It was played in Egypt for at least 3,000 years. This senet set is made of blue faience, a special type of glazed pottery.

- A game of senet could be played on simple squares drawn out in a dusty yard, or scratched onto a slab of stone. It could also be played on the finest boards, like this one, which was fit for a king.

- A senet board had thirty squares, or houses. Some of them were marked with numbers or with good or bad luck signs, rather like our game of snakes and ladders.

- Two players joined in this game. They had seven pieces each. Instead of dice, they threw numbered sticks or small bones before making a move. After the game, they could put their gaming pieces back in the drawer.

FACT FILE

Discovered: Thebes (Luxor), Egypt

Found today: Brooklyn Museum, New York, USA

Date: 1390–1353 BCE (New Kingdom)

Materials: Glazed pottery (faience), partly restored with plaster

Size: 8¼ in (21 cm) long, 3 in (7.7 cm) wide, 2 in (5.5 cm) deep

- Experts have come up with rules for exactly how this game might have been played, but we cannot know for sure.

- This senet board is marked with the name of Amenhotep III (*Ah-men-ho-tep*), a pharaoh who reigned around 4,000 years ago. It was found in his tomb.

- The Egyptians thought that a dead person's journey to the next world must be rather like a game of chance. This is why senet boards were often placed in tombs.

THE CAT GODDESS

◆ Bastet was an Egyptian cat goddess. This statue of Bastet is made of solid bronze. Her eyes are set in gold and her ears are pierced for wearing earrings.

◆ The goddess Bastet originally took the form of a fierce warrior lioness. But over the ages she became much more tame and changed into the cat woman pictured here.

◆ This little statue would have been given to a temple as an offering by one of Bastet's followers. It was found at a city called Bubastis, which was the main center of cat worship.

◆ Bastet was the goddess of childbirth. This is because cats are known to have lots of kittens. The goddess's own kittens are at her feet here.

◆ The sistrum in Bastet's right hand was a kind of rattle. On its handle is the face of Hathor, the goddess of music. A model cat also sits inside the handle.

◆ In her left hand, Bastet carries the top of a menat. This was a necklace of clacking beads worn by entertainers. Bastet was very much a goddess of festivals and fun.

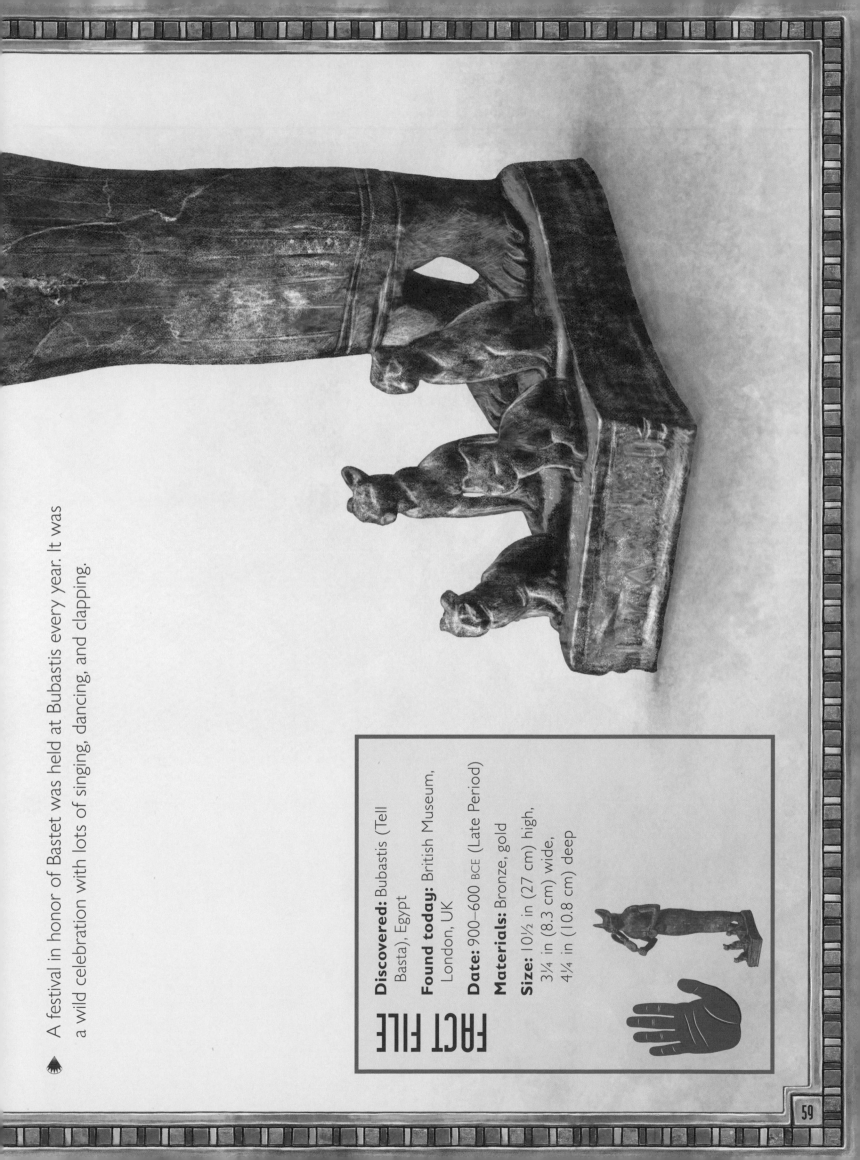

● A festival in honor of Bastet was held at Bubastis every year. It was a wild celebration with lots of singing, dancing, and clapping.

FACT FILE

Discovered: Bubastis (Tell Basta), Egypt

Found today: British Museum, London, UK

Date: 900–600 BCE (Late Period)

Materials: Bronze, gold

Size: 10½ in (27 cm) high, 3¼ in (8.3 cm) wide, 4¼ in (10.8 cm) deep

GOLDEN SANDALS

- The pharaoh Tutankhamun (*Tut-ank-amun*) was only nineteen years old when he died. These sandals were placed on his feet before his body was mummified. The priests chanted prayers and spells at the same time.

- The sandals were crafted to look as if they were everyday footwear made from leather. But they were made of solid gold.

- After his death, Tutankhamun had to travel on to the next world. His golden sandals were supposed to protect him on the journey.

- These sandals look as if the pharaoh's feet were in perfect shape. But in real life Tutankhamun had a serious bone disease that gave him a deformed foot.

FACT FILE

Discovered: Near Thebes (Luxor), Egypt

Found today: Grand Egyptian Museum, Giza, Egypt

Date: About 1327 BCE (New Kingdom)

Material: Gold

Size: Sandals 11½ in (29.5 cm) long, 4 in (10.3 cm) wide

As well as these sandals, the golden caps pictured below were carefully placed over the dead pharaoh's toes. This was to protect them. His body had to be preserved so that the gods could bring it back to life in the next world.

Tutankhamun's tomb was full of golden objects. This precious metal is easy to hammer, shape, and polish until it shines like the sun.

Gold is the perfect material for a royal burial, because it doesn't rust or rot, but lasts forever. When Tutankhamun's mummy was unwrapped, some of the body was damaged, but not those parts protected by gold.

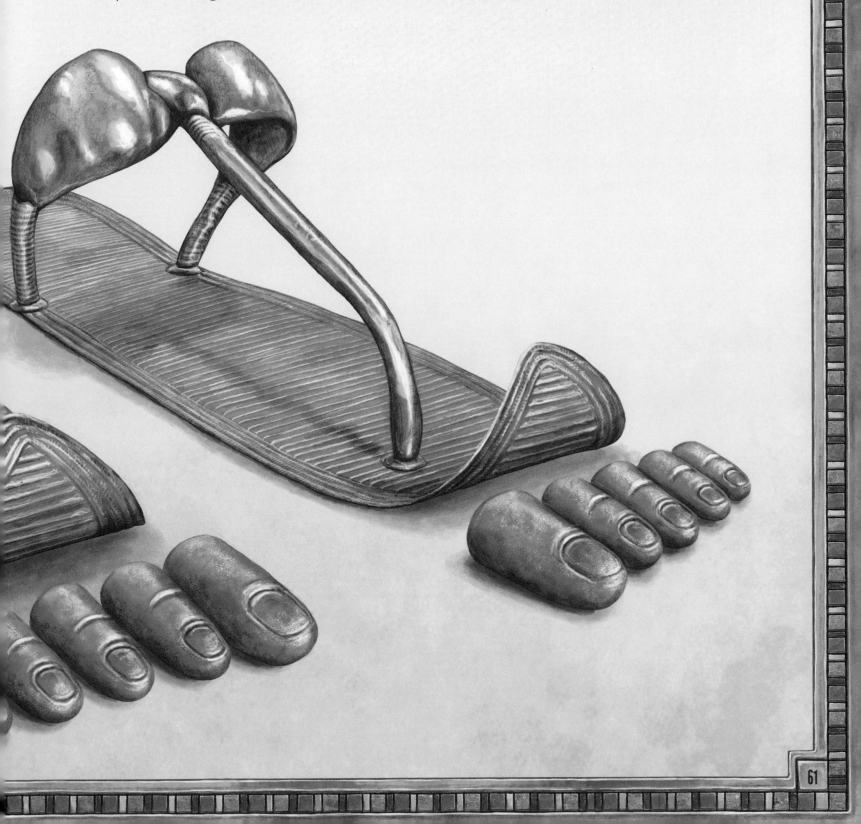

FEAST FOR A PRINCESS

- This picture of Princess Nefertiabet (*Neffer-tia-bet*) was painted on a stone in her tomb at Giza. It is more than 4,500 years old.

- Princess Nefertiabet may have been a priestess of Seshat (*Sesh-at*), the goddess of writing and knowledge. She wears a leopard-skin robe, just like the goddess.

- The picture shows the feast the princess can expect when her spirit reaches the next world.

- Nefertiabet is reaching toward, a table full of crusty loaves. Tasty offerings such as duck, goose, beef, and beer surround the table.

- The boxes at the top list all the good things the princess will enjoy in the afterlife. These include dates, figs, wine, fruit, makeup, incense, and oils.

 **FACT FILE**

Discovered: Giza, near modern Cairo, Egypt

Found today: The Louvre museum, Paris, France

Date: About 2550 BCE (Old Kingdom)

Materials: Limestone, paint

Size: 15 in (38 cm) high, 20½ in (52.5 cm) wide

The writing in the boxes is made up of little pictures and signs, which we call hieroglyphs. Nefertiabet's name is written in hieroglyphs above her head. It means "beautiful one from the east".

The box on the right lists the finest linen cloths being offered to the princess. She will have enough of everything she needs to live forever.

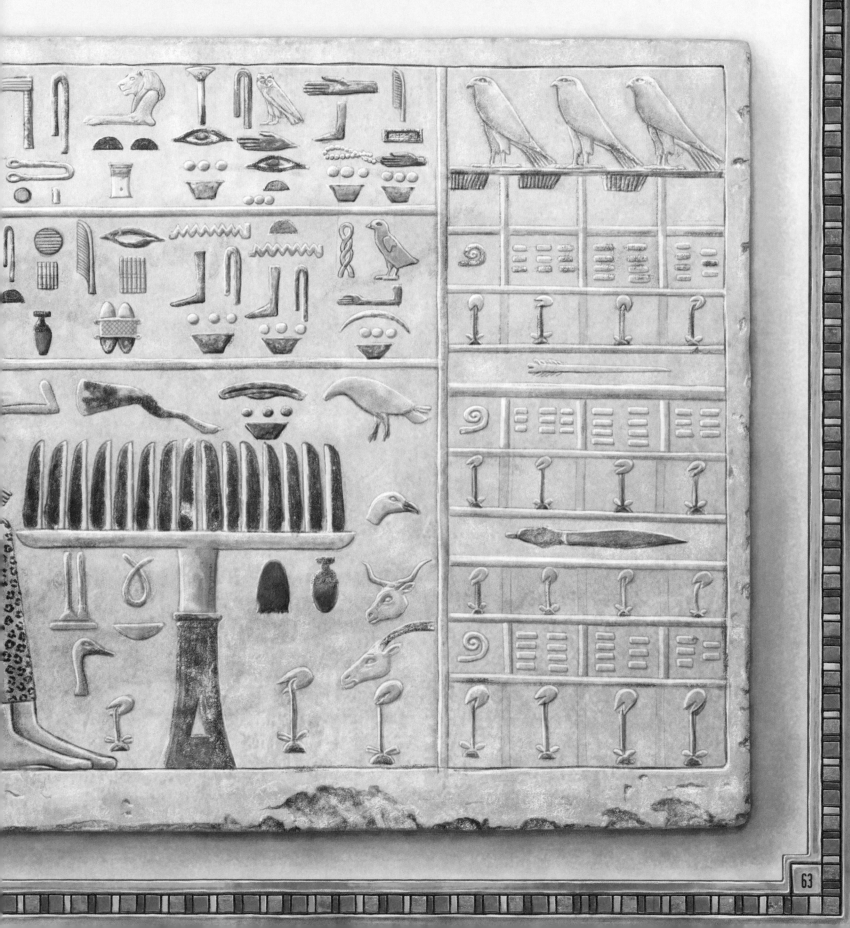

THE RAM GOD

- With its curving horns and woolly coat, this statue of a ram represents the god Amun. It is carved from granite, a hard, gray stone. Amun was one of the most important of all Egyptian gods.

- This statue was found at Kawa, in a region known as Nubia. Several temples and shrines were built there in honor of the ram god, Amun.

- The writing around the side of the statue is in little symbols called hieroglyphs. They read, "The Son of Amun and Mut, Lady of Heaven, who fully satisfies the heart of his father Amun." Mut (*Moot*) was Amun's wife.

- The figure sheltering between the ram's forelegs is the pharaoh Taharqo (*Ta-harr-ko*). He is the "Son of Amun" that the writing on the statue describes. Taharqo came from Nubia, where the statue was discovered.

FACT FILE

Discovered: Kawa, Sudan

Found today: British Museum, London, UK

Date: 690–664 BCE (Late Period)

Material: Granite

Size: 41¾ in (106 cm) high, 24¾ in (63 cm) wide, 64 in (163 cm) cm long

This statue is sometimes called a sphinx. In ancient Egypt, a sphinx was a mythical figure, part animal and part human. Statues of sphinxes usually show them lying down.

A GODDESS'S RATTLE

◆ The great temples of Egypt were filled with clouds of incense and echoed with chanting and music. Priestesses worshipped the gods using musical instruments like this sistrum.

◆ Using a sistrum was a bit like shaking a rattle or tambourine. A priestess shook her sistrum to a rhythm, and the metal disks jingle-jangled in time.

◆ This sistrum is made of a bronze hoop attached to a handle. Its disks are mounted on two wire rods.

◆ Instruments like this sistrum had been played in Egypt for thousands of years before this one was made. Earlier designs often had a boxshape.

◆ The sistrum was especially important in the worship of Hathor, who was the great Egyptian mother goddess. She was also the goddess of music, dancing, joy, and love.

◆ Hathor's head appears on the handle of this sistrum. She was often shown as a cow, with cow's ears, or wearing a horned headdress.

- Ancient Egyptian pharaohs carried a sistrum when they made offerings to the mother goddess, Hathor.

- A model of a cat has been added to this sistrum. It sits above Hathor's head on the handle. The goddess sometimes took the form of a cat.

FACT FILE

Discovered: Possibly Nile delta, Egypt

Found today: Egyptian Museum of Barcelona, Spain

Date: 715–332 BCE (Late Period)

Material: Bronze

Size: 12 in (30 cm) high

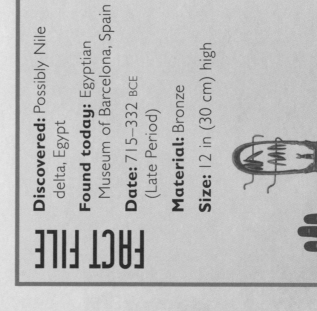

ROYAL BRACELET

- When the mummy of Queen Ahhotep I (*Ah-hotep*) was discovered, this piece of jewelery was found tangled in her hair. It was too small to be a crown, but was just the right size to be worn around her upper arm.

- The bird on the front is a vulture and represents the goddess Nekhbet. She was the protector of Upper Egypt.

- This bracelet is made of gold and set with gemstones. The deep blue stone is lapis lazuli. This precious stone was not found in Egypt. It was mined thousands of miles away in Afghanistan.

- The blue-green stone is called turquoise. It was mined in the Sinai Desert in eastern Egypt and at some other sites in the area.

- Carnelian is the name of the red stone, which was mined in ancient Egypt. It was less precious than lapis or turquoise. Its fiery color reminded the Egyptians of the sun god, Ra.

- The name Ahmose appears on the bracelet. This warrior pharaoh was Ahhotep's son. The queen is said to have helped to rule Egypt while Ahmose was away fighting.

FACT FILE

Discovered: Dra' Abu el-Naga, Thebes, Egypt

Found today: Grand Egyptian Museum, Giza, Egypt

Date: 1560–1530 BCE (Second Intermediate Period)

Materials: Gold, lapis lazuli, turquoise, carnelian

Size: 3 in (7.2 cm) high, 2½ in (6.6 cm) wide

BOOK OF THE DEAD

➤ This painting tells a story. You can read the pictures and hieroglyphs, or picture writing, in the same way as a modern comic strip. But the story they tell is deadly serious.

➤ The scene belongs to a collection of written spells that today we call a Book of the Dead. These spells were often placed in tombs. They were meant to help the dead person pass various tests as they made their way to the afterlife.

➤ In the picture, a royal official called Hunefer has died and is being led by the hand by the jackal-headed god, Anubis.

- Anubis places Hunefer's heart on a pair of scales and weighs it against the Feather of Truth. If his heart is pure, it will be as light as the feather, and Hunefer can go forward.

- If Hunefer's heart is heavy with evil, it will be devoured by a she-demon called Ammit, who is part crocodile, lion, and hippopotamus.

- After Hunefer passes the test, the falcon-headed god Horus (*Haw-rus*) leads him to the throne of Osiris (*Oh-sy-ris*). This god is the judge of all humans and rules the next world.

FACT FILE

Discovered: Thebes (Luxor), Egypt

Found today: British Museum, London, UK

Date: About 1275 BCE (New Kingdom)

Materials: Papyrus, ink, paint

Size: 15¾ in (40 cm) high, 31¼ in (79.3 cm) wide

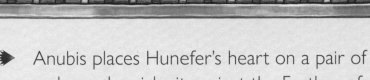

THE SPIRIT OF THE KING

◆ When archaeologists opened up the tomb of Tutankhamun (*Tut-ank-amun*), they saw two men marching toward them. But these weren't real people. They were two life-sized wooden statues.

◆ This is one of the statues. It looks like an armed soldier guarding Tutankhamun's tomb. In reality, the figure is meant to represent the pharaoh himself.

◆ The statue's striped headdress is a symbol of royalty. The rearing cobra at the front stands for the cobra goddess Wedjat, who protected the pharaohs.

◆ Black resin coats the figure's wooden body. His staring eyes are rimmed with bronze, and the clothes he wears are made of shining gold.

◆ The figure wears a kilt and carries a staff. In his right hand he grips a mace, which is a kind of war club that symbolized royal power and bravery.

◆ The ancient Egyptians believed that figures like this one contained the king's life force, which lived on after his death. They called this spirit the *ka*.

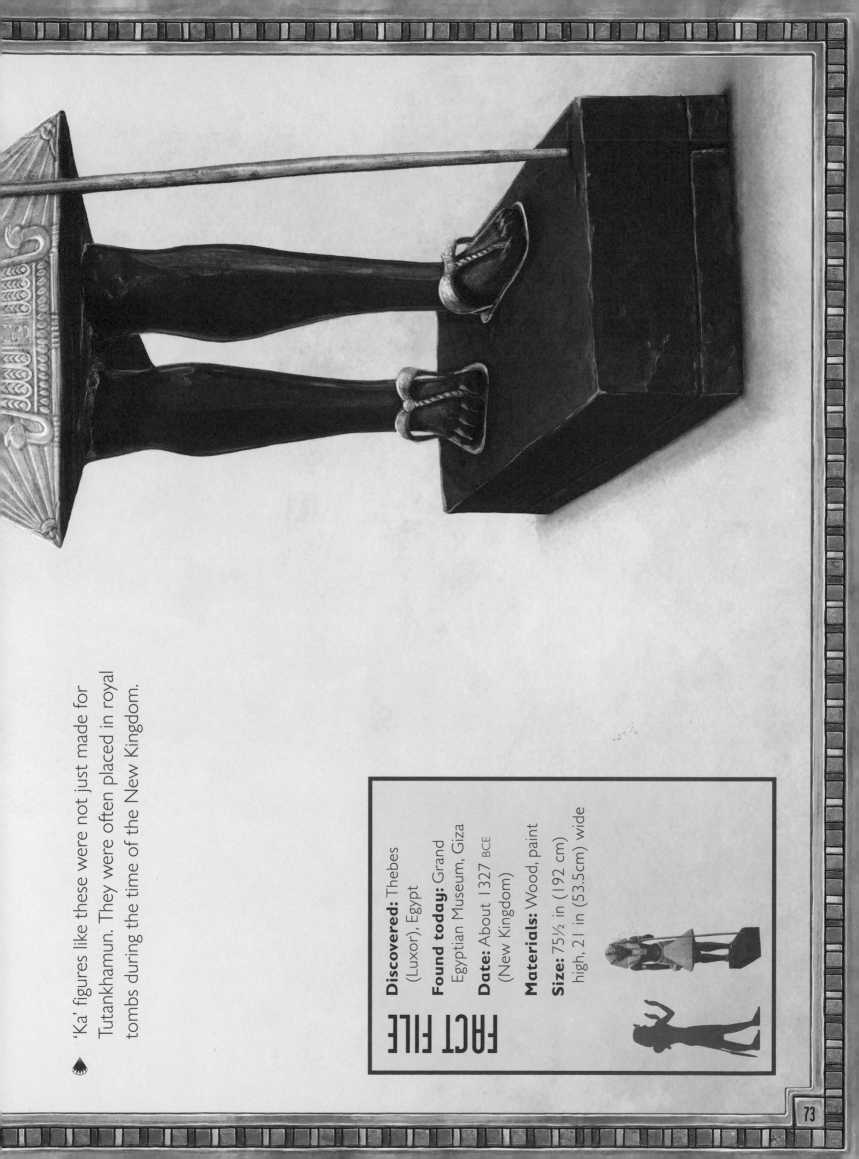

◆ 'Ka' figures like these were not just made for Tutankhamun. They were often placed in royal tombs during the time of the New Kingdom.

FACT FILE

Discovered: Thebes (Luxor), Egypt

Found today: Grand Egyptian Museum, Giza

Date: About 1327 BCE (New Kingdom)

Materials: Wood, paint

Size: 75½ in (192 cm) high, 21 in (53.5cm) wide

THE BLUE HEDGEHOG

➤ Hedgehogs are little animals with spines on their backs. They eat beetles and other insects. If they are attacked, they can roll up into a spiky ball. The ancient Egyptians made models of hedgehogs like this one.

➤ Models of hedgehogs were placed in tombs. This little hedgehog was found in a tomb at Abydos, and might be about 3,500 years old.

- Model hedgehogs in tombs represent the human journey to the afterlife. These animals hibernate over winter and sleep so deeply. they look as if they are dead. When they wake in spring, it is as if they have come alive again.

- This little hedgehog is modeled in blue faience, which is a special type of glazed pottery. The color blue linked the animal to the gods, which is why many model hedgehogs were made in this color.

- Hedgehogs are not harmed by the venom of snakes and scorpions. The Egyptians took this as a sign that hedgehogs are lucky.

- The ancient Egyptians made hedgehog amulets, or lucky charms, hedgehog rattles, and even hedgehog-shaped perfume jars.

FACT FILE

Discovered: Abydos, Egypt

Found today: Ashmolean Museum, Oxford, UK

Date: 1550–1292 BCE (New Kingdom)

Material: Glazed pottery (faience)

Size: 3 in (7.8 cm) long, 2¾ in (6.8 cm) wide

FARMING BY THE NILE

- In the time of the ancient Egyptians, the Nile used to flood each year. Thick, rich mud was left along its banks, which was perfect for growing grains such as corn and barley. These scenes show people farming in fields near the river.

- This wall painting comes from the tomb of an official called Unsu. His job was to oversee the sowing and harvesting of grain for the temple of Amun, god of the sun and the air.

- Before painting, the artist covered the wall with *muna*, a mixture of mud and chopped straw. Plaster was spread on top to create a smooth surface for painting on.

- In the bottom picture, men are digging over the soil with hoes. Others are pulling a simple wooden plow. A sower scatters seeds.

- The middle picture shows laborers harvesting the tall crop. They are cutting off the ears of grain with sickles, leaving the stalks for animals to eat. Women are picking up any fallen grain.

FACT FILE

Discovered: Thebes (Luxor), Egypt

Found today: The Louvre Museum, Paris, France

Date: About 1450 BCE (New Kingdom)

Materials: Plaster, paint

Size: 26¾ in (68 cm) high, 37 in (94 cm) wide

In the top picture, men carry baskets of grain away from the fields. They tip the grain out to be trampled by oxen. This will separate the seeds inside from the husks, or outer shells.

The ancient Egyptians used grain crops like those in this painting to make bread, porridge, and beer. They also grew onions, beans, cabbages, and leeks.

THE PHARAOH'S DAGGERS

➤ These two daggers belonged to the pharaoh Tutankhamun (*Tut-ank-amun*). The dagger above has a blade of precious gold, while the dagger below has a blade of very special iron. Both knives were discovered in the pharaoh's tomb.

➤ The golden blade was engraved with flowers and a diamond pattern. Tutankhamun's name is written on the handle, which is decorated with gold, gemstones, and glass.

➤ Two falcons on the handle of the golden dagger hold a symbol called *shen*. This ancient Egyptian sign looks like a circle of rope. Like an unbroken circle, it represents wholeness and everlasting protection.

➤ The golden dagger was placed on Tutankhamun's mummy because the priests believed it would protect the pharaoh after his death.

- Scientists have discovered that the metal in the iron blade came from outer space. The metalworkers who made it used iron from a meteor that had fallen to Earth.

- The iron dagger's handle was made of gold and was beautifully decorated. The pommel, or knob at the end of the handle, was made of rock crystal.

- Sheaths of shining gold were made to protect each dagger blade.

FACT FILE

Discovered: Near Thebes (Luxor), Egypt

Found today: Grand Egyptian Museum, Giza, Egypt

Date: About 1330 BCE (New Kingdom)

Materials: Gold, iron

Size: Gold dagger 12½ in (31.8 cm) long; Iron dagger 13½ in (34.2 cm) long

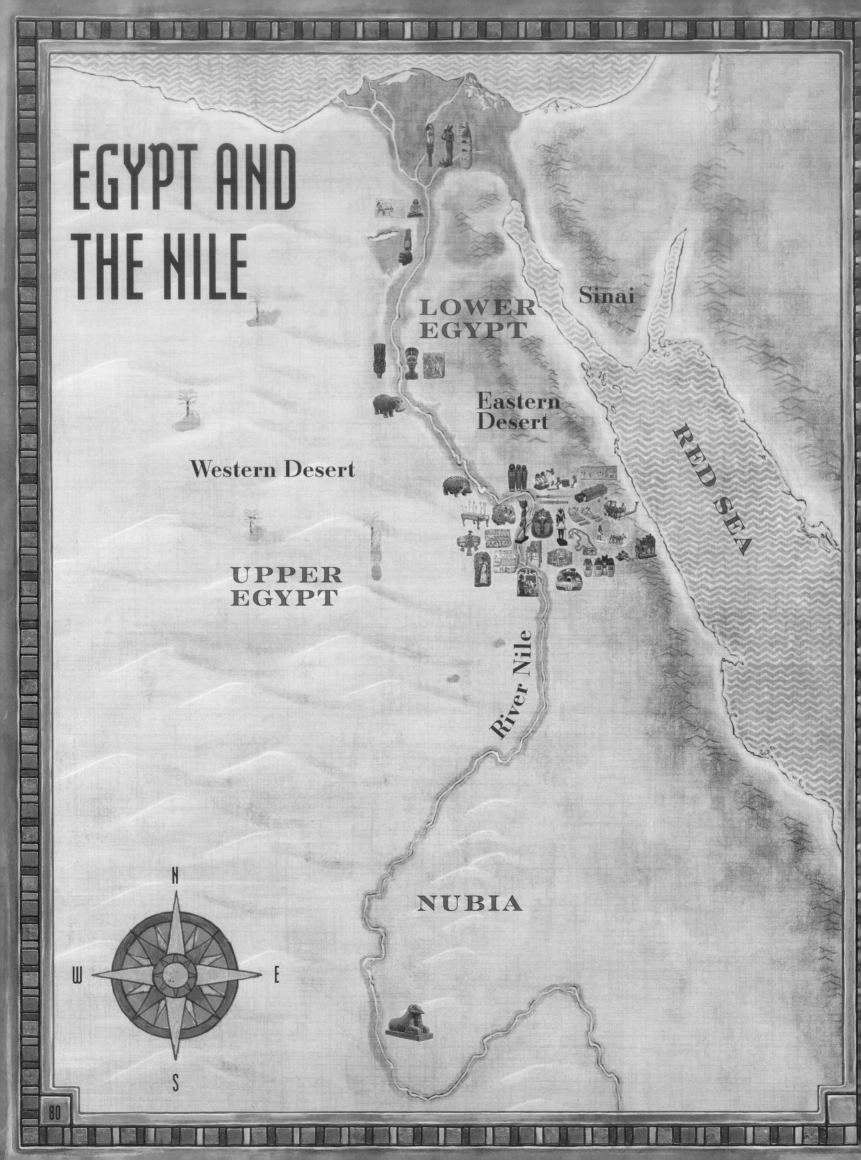

EGYPT AND THE NILE

LOWER EGYPT

Sinai

Eastern Desert

Western Desert

RED SEA

UPPER EGYPT

River Nile

NUBIA

N

W   E

S